Animals
DAY
and
NIGHT

by Jenna Lee Gleisner

amicus readers

Mankato, Minnesota

Ideas for Parents and Teachers

Amicus Readers let children practice reading informational texts at the earliest reading levels. Familiar words and concepts with close photo-text matches support early readers.

Before Reading

- Discuss the cover photo with the child. What does it tell him?
- Ask the child to predict what she will learn in the book.

Read the Book

- "Walk" through the book and look at the photos. Let the child ask questions.
- Read the book to the child, or have the child read independently.

After Reading

- Use the photo quiz at the end of the book to review the text.
- Prompt the child to make connections. Ask: *Are your pets nocturnal or diurnal?*

Amicus Readers are published by Amicus
P.O. Box 1329, Mankato, MN 56002
www.amicuspublishing.us

Library of Congress Cataloging-in-Publication Data

Gleisner, Jenna Lee.
  Animals day and night / Jenna Lee Gleisner.
    pages cm. -- (Animal Antonyms)
  Includes bibliographical references and index.
  ISBN 978-1-60753-505-8 (hardcover : alk. paper) --
ISBN 978-1-60753-531-7 (eBook)
  1. English language--Synonyms and antonyms-
-Juvenile literature. 2. English language--
Comparison--Juvenile literature. 3. Animals--
Juvenile literature. I. Title.
  PE1591.G553 2014
  428.1--dc23
                           2013004515

Photo Credits: Hemera/Thinkstock, cover (top back); Shutterstock Images, cover (top front), 1 (top), 6, 7, 16 (bottom middle); Thinkstock, cover (bottom back), 11, 16 (top right); iStockphoto, cover (bottom front), 12; Cejen/Shutterstock Images, 1 (bottom); Krivosheev Vitaly/Shutterstock Images, 3; John Carnemolla/Shutterstock Images, 4, 16 (top left); Jupiterimages/Thinkstock, 5; Kirk Geisler/Shutterstock Images, 8, 16 (bottom left); S.Cooper Digital/Shutterstock Images, 9; Vitaly Ilyasov/Shutterstock Images, 10, 16 (bottom right); Gerald Marella/Shutterstock Images, 13; Guy J. Sagi/Shutterstock Images, 14; Ivan Kuzmin/Shutterstock Images, 15, 16 (top middle)

Produced for Amicus by The Peterson Publishing Company and Red Line Editorial

Editor Jenna Gleisner
Designer Jake Nordby
Printed in the United States of America
Mankato, MN
July, 2013
PA1938
10 9 8 7 6 5 4 3 2 1

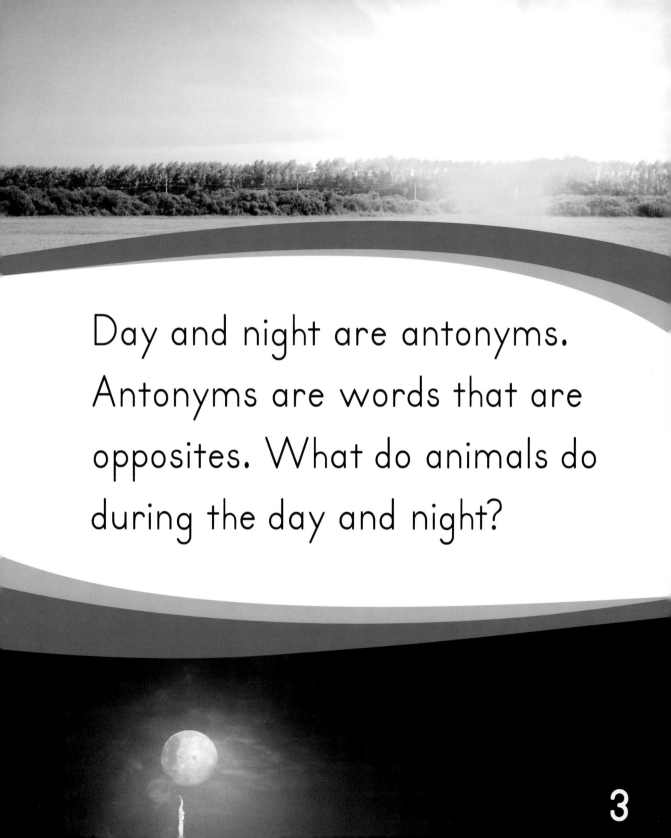

Day and night are antonyms. Antonyms are words that are opposites. What do animals do during the day and night?

The sun rises to start the day. At dawn, roosters crow good morning.

The moon comes out at night. Coyotes howl at the moon.

The sun shines during the day. Lizards lie in bright sunlight.

The moon shines at night.
Owls look for food
in the moonlight.

It is warm during
the day. Moose swim
to cool off.

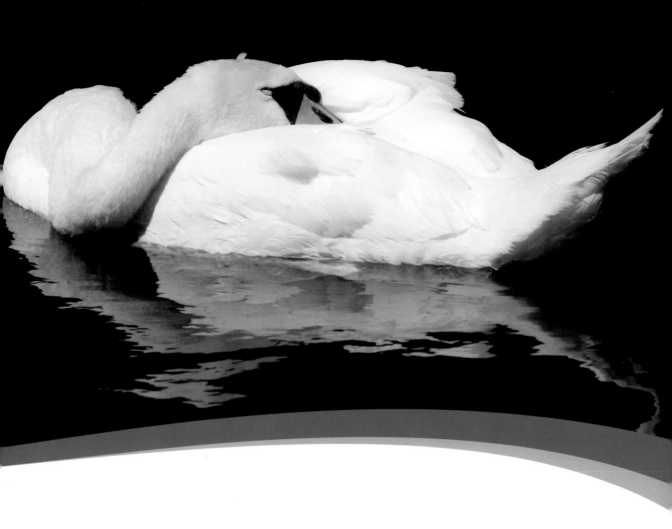

It is cold at night.
Swans sleep with their
bills tucked under their
feathers to keep warm.

Diurnal animals are active during the day. Squirrels gather nuts during the day.

Nocturnal animals are active at night. Beavers build dams at night.

Nocturnal animals
sleep during the day.
Beavers sleep after
building their dams.

Diurnal animals sleep at night. Squirrels sleep at night after gathering nuts.

The sun goes down at
the end of the day.
Deer return to their beds
at dusk to end the day.

In a cave, bats are
just waking up.
What do you do in the
day and at night?

Photo Quiz

Which animals are active during the day?
Which animals are active at night?